'Ecila Mai' means 'I am Alice' spelled backwards. The name reminds the author to recognize different perspectives and to appreciate different points of view. She was born in Philadelphia, Pennsylvania and raised in Baltimore, Maryland. She has been writing poems all of her life. Her grandmother, Alice Carroll Griffin taught her to treasure her family, believe in God and to always "own your own home". Her mother, Hazel Lloyd Leslie taught her to think before you speak, pronounce your words correctly and read to gain knowledge. As a result of their influence, she graduated from the University of Maryland, College Park, married her true love, Eric Andre Brooks (her dearly departed husband), raised a family, and owns her own home. She believes, in Christ, all things work together for good.

This book is dedicated to my children, Jason and Jaime, son-in-law, Christopher, and my grandchildren, Jeremiah, Justin, and Jaxon and bonus grandson, Darian. I love them dearly and pray that their own epiphanies will bless them to express themselves in passionate, compassionate, and artistic ways.

Ecila Mai

HAIKUS-ISMS

AUSTIN MACAULEY PUBLISHERS®
LONDON • CAMBRIDGE • NEW YORK • SHARJAH

Ordering Information
Quantity sales: Special discounts are available on quantity purchases by corporations, associations, and others. For details, contact the publisher at the address below.

Publisher's Cataloging-in-Publication data
Mai, Ecila
Haikus-isms

ISBN 9798886932072 (Paperback)
ISBN 9798886932089 (ePub e-book)

www.austinmacauley.com/us

First Published 2024
Austin Macauley Publishers LLC
40 Wall Street 33rd Floor, Suite 3302
New York, NY 10005
USA

mail-usa@austinmacauley.com
+1 (646) 5125767

I want to acknowledge and thank my family and friends who have supported me in this endeavor and listened and encouraged me to keep on writing and being myself. I, especially thank my daughter for her assistance with the detail.

A poem in three lines
Five, Seven, Five Syllables
Less said, much revealed

Emergence

One day I grew up
No one ever stays the same
Life keeps on changing

One day I knew me
No hiding from my true self
I am who I am

One day in a dream
I was as free as a bird
A phoenix took flight

One day it happens
Needing no one's approval
We learn to move on

One day I heard it
An inner voice was speaking
Write the poetry

One day in the sky
I imagined God above
I cried tears of joy

One day at a time
I strive to treasure rainbows
Not dwell on rainstorms

Enlightenment

Just when life gets rough
Changing course made things better
And peace will prevail

Just when the rain stops
The sky beckons to the clouds
The sun is coming

Just when all is lost
A new day gives new meaning
A fresh start brings hope

Just when the joy leaves
I remember gratitude
I count the blessings

Just when the truth hurts
I realize there's something worse
Lies can feel good too

Just when time runs out
Presumptively while there's breath
Destiny can change

Just when doubts set in
Praying for a way to cope
Removes many fears

Evolution

When love has a place
Compassion enters the room
Kindness fills the house

Joy is a good thing
Joy is such a game changer
Joy makes you happy

Kindness is a path
Kindness always makes a way
It will open doors

Peace is everything
In Christ, my mind is at rest
In Him, all is well

Truth cannot be bound
Like a cactus in the sun
It reaches for light

Sometimes we will cry
Life is not always carefree
We deal with troubles

Sorrow masks the heart
While good days cover the hurt
Bright smiles hide the pain

Environment

The rain is falling
Tears flow in the wind unseen
Nature heals my soul

The sun is shining
Memories burn in the heat
Flames flicker and fade

Under the moonlight
Even in the dark forest
Shadows leap and dance

Leaves falling from trees
Butterflies leaving cocoons
Seasons are changing

Where does life begin?
Where are fireflies at dawn?
Where do thoughts come from?

Winds do blow over
Broken branches force new limbs
Buds grow into leaves

Snowflakes are falling
The horizon glistening
It's a bright winter

Essentials

I enjoy reading
Seeing places never been
Joy's in the pages

Happiness is joy
I do not mind you smiling
Laughter frees the soul

I'm free; so I thought
Then I saw ants scattering
Freedoms are not free

The rhythms flowing
My mind dances to the beat
Dwelling in the past

One day is enough
To dream away a lifetime
Lost in fantasy

Talking to myself
Seeking for the right answer
Finding more questions

Art does speak to me
So poetic and pleasing
Draws me, without words

Empowerment

I hope that one day
We treat each other kindly
Before it's too late

I hope for real peace
Children are not born to hate
They deserve better

I hope for your joy
Cool breezes in the sunshine
Iced tea in crystal

I hope for good health
My mind in charge of itself
Strong and graceful limbs

I hope goodness thrives
So much so, it's overwhelms
So happy, can't breathe

I hope love prevails
Joy, happiness and big smiles
I hope to grow old

I hope for no pain
Dying while I dream in bed
Happy and carefree

Enamored

Found in fairy tales
Pots of gold and three wishes
Over the rainbow

Rain while the sun shines
The sprinklings from foggy mists
Splashes at the pool

Laying in the grass
Barefoot, bearing private thoughts
No holding back now

There's great depth to love
It's endless and limitless
Beyond infinite

Love's warmth surrounds us
Like the sun brightly shining
As hearts melt and fill

When new birth happens
Not a happier moment
Then a second chance

Smiling and giggling
Remembering special things
Having a good time

Entitlement

Children running wild
Love them laughing at themselves
Free from fears and doubts

The realization
Freedom has never been free
It's quite expensive

When it's a feeling
My mind is free to believe
Feelings often change

We're free to choose love
Love does not always choose us
Still, love is worth it

Pain lasts a long time
Sorrow slowly fades away
But hurt does linger

The truth cannot lie
Your shadow cannot leave you
And time cannot stop

I'm not a mistake
Although I will make mistakes
It's as it should be

Evidence

Either you do care
Or nothing really matters
But you must own it

My eyes search for truth
Looking beyond appearance
That seen and unseen

Life's a rocky road
The twists and turns never stop
Until your road ends

Each day begins anew
A fresh start, another chance
Yesterday is gone

I could not go there
Way down deep inside myself
Where there's no hiding

Clinched eyes stop the tears
Smiles work to hide the sorrow
My face betrays me

Reality check
Attitude changes the game
It is what it is

Engagement

After the storm ends
A calm cool soft breeze whispers
It will be alright

Through the darkest day
In the blackest of dark night
His light always shines

Awake and arise
Morning dew drips wet and fresh
Birds sing and bees buzz

Thoughts of brighter days
Spring is my true heart's desire
A time filled with hope

Won't go out today
Winter freezes the house pipes
I stay in my bed

The leaves change and fall
Autumn withers on the vine
The beach is now closed

It's too hot to think
No comfort in the sunshine
Even shade is hot

Emphatically

Racism is wrong
To be most perfectly clear
There's one human race

At the very least
To be most perfectly clear
God is ultimate

We age from day one
To be most perfectly clear
Innocence will not last

Once in a lifetime
To be most perfectly clear
You are perfection

When you've seen it all
To be most perfectly clear
You still don't know much

There's not much to do
To be most perfectly clear
If you don't want growth

The more things will change
To be most perfectly clear
The same things remain

Economically

Wealth is not money
To be rich is to have friends
Ones that support you

A good name is gold
Freedom is to be yourself
It is all that's yours

Invest in yourself
Stress less, Bless more, Be happy
Your health is your wealth

Treasure those you love
Like a cherished precious jewel
Treat them like diamonds

A day is a gift
Filled with opportunities
Every moment counts

Beauty does not fade
It increases with each day
It's inside, not out

In all things give thanks
Trust Him with all that you have
God gave it to you

Expenses

It's your decision
What your choices will cost you
Benefit or lost

A choice can cost you
Spend your life paying for it
Full price, no returns

When they're used wisely
Their value tends to increase
Talent and time

They are yours to have
The choices are numerous
The outcome, just one

If the choice is wrong
A choice can be expensive
With lifetime payments

If the choice is right
The outcome could still be wrong
But who really knows

Nobody wants them
The pay-down payments' payoff
Yet nothing is free

Exceptions

Being calm and cool
Despite the circumstances
Takes strong inner peace

The depth of courage
And confidence is great when
The mind is certain

The reach of great calm
Over real calamity
Conquers confusion

Smile and don't worry
Despite your problems give thanks
Be patient and pray

Though the world seems harsh
It's not meant to be easy
It's meant for courage

When all things begin
Anything is possible
Time seems so endless

When things end badly
Everything is difficult
Time seems so draining

Endings

Each life has chapters
Everyone their own story
Everyone their time

A page is one page
Pages do not define you
You define the page

We make the chapters
The chapters make the story
Living makes the book

My life has pages
Each line my experience
Each word important

What we least expect
Life, love and sorrow will end
In time, we move on

Fresh or tattered page
Some truths revealed, some are not
Hidden between lines

We need only search
To know who we really are
The contents within